VIDYA ARVIND

Heal Your Life

Heal & Transform By Following The Satvic Way Of Living

Thank You Babe! my better half
Thank You Akshaya my lovely daughter :)
Thank You Family
Thank You God
Thanks to all the spiritual masters, angels and sapta rishis
Thank You Guruji Krishnananda and Guruji Amara
Thank You "The Satvic Movement Team"
Thank You "SynchroShakthi" – Ms.Karthika Nair
Thank You to all the people who are reading my book
Lot's Of Gratitude!!!!!!

Let there be Love, Light and Healing In everyone's life. Let us transform this kali yuga to satya yuga with good health.

Contents

Acknowledgement

Writing a book is a journey that involves the support and encouragement of numerous individuals and entities. As I reflect on the completion of "Heal Your Life," I am filled with profound gratitude for the invaluable contributions of those who have played a part in bringing this project to fruition.

First and foremost, I would like to express my deepest appreciation to my family for their unwavering love, patience, and understanding throughout the writing process. Their belief in me and their constant encouragement provided the foundation upon which this book was built. I am eternally grateful for their support.

I am also indebted to the countless mentors, teachers, and guides who have imparted their knowledge and wisdom to me over the years. Your insights have enriched my understanding and shaped the ideas presented in this book. I am deeply grateful for your guidance and mentorship which made me cure my hyperthyroid and now completely healthy and for the purpose of sharing this knowledge to the entire world.

1

Introduction

This book is going to change your Life in a positive way.

Here we are going to learn about

1. How to maintain good health
2. Satvic Lifestyle
3. How to reverse your illness
4. How to Lose weight
5. Pranic Healing through powerful meditation
6. How to resolve conflicts in relationship
7. Gratitude and Surrendering to the higher power
8. Step by step guide to achieve Satvic Lifestyle in 21 days
9. Taking a wellness test after 21 days and 3 months to see how you miraculously reversed your illness.
10. Who are my masters and resources

2

Chapter 1

How To Achieve Good Health

Let's understand about our Human Body. It is made up of 5 elements. Earth (plant foods growing out of earth), Air, Fire, Water, Akasha (Sky).Any Imbalance with one or more of these elements will lead to illness.

A Human with Good Health will have a perfect balance of these 5 elements.For a healthy person he would be able to do the following:

1. Bowels getting cleared in the morning everyday
2. Ideal BMI
3. Clear Skin
4. Feeling Energetic throughout the day
5. Experience strong sense of Hunger 1-2 times a day
6. Getting Deep sleep in 2 to 5 minutes

7. No pain in the body
8. Will have a smiling face and a positive aura
9. Wakes up without snoozing the alarm and feels excited to wake up
10. Easily letting go of unpleasant things
11. Will not get easily angry
12. Selfless love for close family and friends

We too can achieve this Good Health through living in a Satvic way.

Humans operate in a combination of 3 modes or Gunas:

1. Satvic
2. Rajasic
3. Tamasic

Satvic Guna: Full of Energy
Rajasic Guna: Full of Passion
Tamasic Guna: Full of Ignorance and Laziness

We need all the 3 gunas to be balanced to have a happy healthy life so we need to keep the Satvic component high, Rajasic medium and Tamasic Guna the lowest or only at night.

So we now know how to have a Healthy Life and now we will dive deeper into practically implying these in our modern busy Life.

3

Chapter 2

Powerful 7 Habits To Reverse Your Health Condition

Habit 1: Having a Clean Body

We all are blessed to have a healer who heals, repairs and cleans our body everyday which is called

Prana Shakti.

Prana Shakti takes 80% of its time to digest our food after which it will heal and clean our body. Unfortunately we always keep our Prana Shakti busy in digestion, which inturn affects us because there is no time left by prana shakti to heal and clean our body.

Let's take an example: We eat Bread butter toast for break-fast,Rice with Dal for lunch,Tea/Coffee with cookies for snacks and Poori Subji for dinner. Next day we put in another load of food to get digested and this continues everyday. This way all the time is taken just to digest our food and there is no time left to heal or clean our body.

Let's understand that there is a fire element in our body which helps in effective digestion of our food.Depending on the position of Sun.During sunset the effectiveness of digestion slows down. Ideally if you finish your dinner by 7pm then the digestion takes 8 hours which means by 3AM in the morning your digestion process is complete and from 3AM to 6AM our prana shakti goes deeper into each organ and removes the toxins through stool,urine,sweat and breath.

We now know how important it is to have your dinner by 7pm. By doing this we can keep our body clean and you will be able to pass your stool without any trouble every morning. Also our prana shakti gets enough time to reverse our health condition and you will feel more energetic with a glowing skin in the long run.

Eat your dinner by 7pm

I would suggest you start having a light dinner like a bowl of soup or a big bowl of salad if you cannot have dinner by 7pm.

You might feel it's impossible to have dinner before 7pm that too a light dinner but understand this is how our ancestors did and they all were healthy and lived a long and happy life.

If you feel hungry after having a light dinner you can drink coconut water, fruits or herbal tea.Trust me it will be rare that you will feel hungry.Also sleep early by 9:30 pm so that you can wake up early and you don't feel hungry late in the night.

Many people call this intermittent fasting.Research is proved that it helps in weight loss and even reverse disease.

Anything to form a habit takes 21 days and if cultivating this habit can give us so many benefits why don't we make this a habit.

Let's Do It!!!!!!

Habit 2: Eat Plant Based Food

*We are all blessed with a beautiful place given by mother earth and she knows what is best for us that's why she has given us **natural fruits and vegetables**.*

We need to understand and be aware of what we eat. Always have this golden rule: anything which comes naturally from mother earth is good for our health and anything that is processed and advertised by TV commercials is not good for our health.

Let's Classify Plant Based and Processed Food.

Plant Based Food	Processed Food
Fruits	Packed chips
Veggies	Frozen smileys
Grains	Tinned and canned food
Nuts and Seeds	Bottled juices and A rated drinks
Sprouts	Pizza
Coconut	Burger
Brown Rice	Lots of sugar and candies

Let's switch to plant based food and see how our body miraculously changes. We will start seeing that we fall sick only once or twice a year which is how it should be for a healthy person.

In Bhagavad Gita it is mentioned that how we eat makes us who we are.

If we eat Plant based Living Wholesome Food we become more Satvic in nature.

If we eat food which is too spicy, salty with lots of masala we become Rajasic in nature.

If we eat meat, fish and spoiled food which we keep for days in the fridge, reheat and eat, we become more Tamasic in nature.

From now on we will be more aware of what we are eating. I know it's difficult to avoid pizzas and coke but always remember our body was not designed to digest food apart from what our mother earth gave.So lets eat healthy food for 3 months to see how our body changes and still if you feel you don't see any changes then go ahead with your current eating habits.But atleast give it a try and be consistent.

Habit 2: Eating Plant Based Food

I would suggest you go to your kitchen and take a big box with a lid. Remove all the packet food, bottled and canned food and read the ingredients for each one and you will know if you still need it or you will throw it in the box. Once you collect all the processed food in the box, close it and label it as not to open for 3 months.

Packaged food has more chemicals than we think. Any food that is cooked more than three hours before being eaten will be liked by people who are in the mode of ignorance (Tamasic) .

To make us get addicted to packaged foods they add sugar,salt and edible oils with lots of chemicals which are deadly for us to consume.

The Red, Green and Yellow List

There are three lists which any food item falls into: Also avoid the 3 whites which are Sugar, Maida and White Rice.

Note: Anything which ends with sugar, ose, syrup and ol is all sugar.Often, these industrial sugars are even worse and addictive than white sugar.

Red List	Yellow List	Green List
Deadly ingredients	Clean ingredients	Ingredients themselves
Highly processed	Minimally processed	Not processed
Never Consume	Consume sometimes	Consume always

Amazing swaps for packaged food:

1. Chips: makhana,homemade popcorn,roasted spiced nuts
2. Chocolates: homemade choco nut bars,chocolate smoothie bowl,homemade chocolate nutties
3. Biscuits: homemade biscuits,coconut slices,fresh fruits
4. Aerated drinks: Fresh homemade juices,fresh coconut water
5. Packaged sauces and dressings: Homemade dips

Buy only fresh fruits and vegetables, Arrange nuts in a transparent jar and keep it on your dining table or any place in your living area. Whenever you feel like munching chips or chocolate you can have nuts and dates instead.

Let's Do It!!!!! Let's Eat Healthy Wholesome Plant Based Food!!!!

Habit 3: Sleep Like A Baby

It is so difficult to sleep in 5 minutes. Ever wondered why ?! It's because we are constantly watching our screens, be it Laptop TV or Mobile phone before going to sleep which emits blue rays which sends a wrong signal to our brain that it is not time to sleep.There is a hormone called melatonin that the brain produces sending a response to darkness.It helps with the timing of your circadian rhythm and with sleep.

If we do high stimulation activity then we feel difficult to sleep and our mind is cluttered with too many thoughts, even when we physically sleep our mind does not sleep.

A deep sleep is very important for our prana shakti to repair and clean our body. During deep sleep our immune system protects us from harmful infection. Our prana shakti also recharges our battery for the next day.Deep sleep is also very important to register whatever we have learnt throughout the day it will transfer from the short term memory to the long term memory which will make us sharper.

At University Of California they researched and discovered that just one night of insufficient sleep can damage cells and make you age quicker.That's how important it is to get deep sleep.

It is between **10pm to 2am** that our prana shakti does the highest recharging so it is important to be in deep sleep during this period.

Now we have learnt the benefits and why and when is deep sleep required. So let's see how to get deep sleep.By switching high stimulation activity to Low stimulation activity we can attain deep sleep and we should have dinner early before 7pm and switch off or keep away our devices by 8pm and for an hour we need to do low stimulation activity and then go to bed by 9pm or 9:30pm max.

Low Stimulation Activity	High Stimulation Activity
1. Meditation or Prayer	1. Watching TV
1. Reading a book	2. Loud music
3. Playing with your kids	3. Playing video games/Looking at your mobile
4. Yoga Nidra Track	4. Working at Laptop

Tip: Switch to Low Stimulation activity 1 hour before going to bed.
Avoid High stimulation activity before going to bed.

Remember a good night's sleep is very important for your well being. See how you can reschedule or manage work timings to get better sleep.

Let's do this!!! Let's sleep on time. We set an example for our children if we follow good habits naturally they will also follow it.

Habit 4: Let's Move Our Body
We are blessed with an amazing human body so let's see how we can celebrate movement.

If we sit for long hours and don't move our bodies for days then

1. Stomach can't secrete digestive juices properly
2. Muscles starts weakening
3. Pancreas can't generate insulin properly
4. Thyroid gland is unable to secrete hormone properly

We all have got comfortable with machines that make it a sedentary lifestyle for us. I have listed down 10 types of exercises, choose one or two of the most you love to do and make it a habit you do it everyday for an hour.

Here are 10 types of exercises that you can incorporate into your everyday routine to promote overall fitness and well-being:

1. Cardiovascular Exercise:
   - Running or jogging
   - Cycling
   - Jump rope
   - High-intensity interval training (HIIT)

2. Strength Training:
   - Body weight exercises (push-ups, squats, lunges)
   - Weightlifting (dumbbells, barbells, resistance bands)
   - Yoga or Pilates for functional strength

3. Flexibility and Mobility:
   - Stretching exercises (dynamic and static)
   - Yoga poses
   - Tai Chi or Qigong for fluid movement

4. Core Workouts:
   - Bicycle crunches and Leg raises

5. Balance Exercises:
   - Single-leg stands
   - Bosu ball exercises
   - Yoga poses that challenge balance

6. Agility Training:
   - Cone drills
   - Ladder drills
   - Shuttle runs

7. Swimming:
   - An excellent full-body workout that is easy on the joints.

8. Climbing:
   ● Indoor or outdoor rock climbing
   ● Climbing stairs for a simpler option

9. Mental Fitness Exercises:
   ● Mindful meditation
   ● Brain-training games
   ● Activities that challenge cognitive skills

10. Active Recreation:
   ● Hiking
   ● Biking
   ● Playing recreational sports (tennis, basketball, soccer)

Remember to consult with a healthcare professional or fitness expert before starting a new exercise routine, especially if you have any existing health concerns or conditions. Additionally, it's essential to listen to your body, start gradually, and progress at a pace that suits your fitness level.

Habit 4: Let's move our Body
Tip: **Be Consistent** . Remember it takes 21 days to form a habit. So be consistent and do the exercise that you love the most.

Habit 5: Enhancing Relationships
We are blessed to have a family who loves us unconditionally

Oftentimes we do not know how to express our feelings with our loved ones. We always throw our stress and frustration on them and we barely listen when they talk to us. It happens to most of us, including me.

But from now on we can pay attention and be aware that we enhance our relationship by giving Love and Respect.

Our Universe always works like this: **What we Give is what we get**.

Here are few things that we can do to enhance our relationship:

Effective Communication:
- Be an active listener.
- Express yourself openly and honestly.
- Use "I" statements to express your feelings without blaming.

Show Appreciation:
- Regularly express gratitude for the positive aspects of the relationship.
- Acknowledge and appreciate each other's efforts and accomplishments.

Quality Time:
- Spend quality time together, free from distractions.
- Engage in activities that you both enjoy.

Empathy:
- Try to understand and validate each other's feelings.
- Put yourself in the other person's shoes to gain perspective.

Respect Boundaries:
- Understand and respect each other's personal space and boundaries.

● Communicate openly about individual needs and expectations.

Conflict Resolution:
● Approach conflicts with a willingness to understand and find solutions.
● Use "I" statements and avoid blaming or criticizing.

Celebrate Achievements:
● Acknowledge and celebrate each other's successes, big or small.
● Share in the joy of accomplishments and milestones.

Shared Goals and Values:
● Identify common goals and values to build a sense of unity.
● Discuss and align long-term aspirations.

Forgiveness:
● Learn to forgive and let go of past grievances.
● Holding onto resentment can hinder relationship growth.

Continuous Growth:
● Encourage personal and mutual growth.
● Support each other's goals and aspirations.

Remember that every relationship is unique, and these tips may need to be adapted to fit the specific dynamics of your connections. Open communication and a willingness to understand and support each other are fundamental keys to successful relationships.

By Enhancing our relationships with our loved ones we can reach our ultimate health and even reverse diseases.

Let's always listen to them with undivided attention and repeat what they said in our words. This way they know that we are listening to them and trying to understand the problem from their perspective.They will now feel safe to open up and begin to trust with their innermost feelings and thoughts.

By practicing this habit it prevents misunderstandings and fights.

Habit 5: Enhancing Relationships
Tip: Seek first to understand before being understood.

Habit 6: A Purpose

Purpose is what drives you to wake up with excitement.

There are 5 blue zones in the world. They have a maximum number of people living up to the age of 100 years in these 5 blue zones. One of the reasons is that they all are very active and they do not retire at the age of 60. They do something that they love the most. They have a purpose when they wake up every morning.

Without purpose we just do our daily chores and go to sleep, which creates a mental block because even after following all the Satvic Lifestyle Habits if we miss this habit we cannot get fully cured from our diseases. Also purpose is something which keeps us motivated and excited about the day.

Determining your purpose in life is a deeply personal and often evolving process. Here are some steps and considerations that may help you discover your purpose:

Self-Reflection:
- Take time for introspection. Reflect on your values, interests, and passions.
- Consider moments in your life when you felt most fulfilled or satisfied.

Identify Strengths and Talents:
- List your strengths, skills, and natural talents.
- Consider activities or tasks that come easily to you and bring you joy.

Set Goals:
- Establish short-term and long-term goals.
- Define what success means to you and what you want to achieve in different areas of your life.

Explore Interests:
- Try new activities and experiences to discover what you enjoy.
- Pay attention to what energizes you and makes you lose track of time.

Consider Impact:
- Think about the impact you want to have on the world or on the lives of others.
- Identify causes or issues that resonate with you.

Seek Inspiration:

● Read books, listen to podcasts, or watch documentaries that inspire and resonate with your values.

● Learn from the experiences of others who have found their purpose.

Ask for Feedback:

● Seek input from friends, family, and mentors about your strengths and what they see as your unique contributions.

● Sometimes, others can see things in us that we might overlook.

Embrace Challenges:

● Challenges and obstacles can provide valuable insights into what truly matters to you.

● Use setbacks as opportunities for growth and self-discovery.

Experiment and Adapt:

● Your purpose may evolve over time. Be open to experimenting with different paths and adapting as needed.

● Allow yourself the flexibility to change course if necessary.

Connect with Others:

● Engage with like-minded individuals or communities.

● Collaborate with others who share your interests and values.

Remember that finding your purpose is not a one-time event but a lifelong journey. It's okay if your sense of purpose evolves as you grow and experience new things. Be patient with yourself, and enjoy the process of self-discovery. If you find it challenging to navigate this journey alone, consider seeking guidance from a counselor, life coach, or mentor.

Let's understand Swadharma,Purpose and Service.

Swadharma =your innate strengths (which you can easily do for eg:singing)

Purpose = your reason for being

Service = fulfilling your purpose to serve others

If we don't align with our innate strengths and do some other work because that gives us more money or status then internal frustration starts building and our prana shakti gets wasted in handling the stress and in turn the health starts deteriorating.

The power of living in accordance with our innate strengths is also beautifully explained in the Bhagavad Gita.

श्रेयान्स्वधर्मो विगुणः परधर्मात्स्वनुष्ठितात् ।

स्वधर्मे निधनं श्रेयः परधर्मो भयावहः ॥ 3.35 ॥

Transliteration:
    śreyān swa-dharmo viguṇaḥ para-dharmāt sv-anuṣṭhitāt
    sva-dharme nidhanaṁ śreyaḥ para-dharmo bhayāvahaḥ

Translation:

"It is far better to discharge one's prescribed duties, even though faultily, than another's duties perfectly. Destruction in the course of performing one's own duty is better than engaging in another's duties, for to follow another's path is dangerous."

In this verse, Lord Krishna is advising Arjuna about the importance of adhering to one's own duties or responsibilities, known as "swadharma." The verse emphasizes the idea that it is better to fail in the pursuit of one's own duties than to succeed in performing the duties of another.

Swadharma vs. Paradharma:

- Swadharma (one's own duty): This refers to the responsibilities and roles that are inherent to an individual based on their position in society, family, or profession.
- Paradharma (another's duty): This involves taking on responsibilities or roles that do not naturally belong to an individual.

In summary, the verse underscores the significance of personal duty and responsibility, suggesting that each individual has a unique role to play in the grand scheme of life. It encourages a focus on one's own path, even if it involves challenges and imperfections, rather than straying onto paths that may seem easier but are not meant for one's personal growth and well-being.

The second important component is Service. When we do something that only serves us then it is considered as a selfish action whereas when we do something that benefits our family and society that's when we are performing the highest service.

If you feel excited to get out of bed in the morning, you look forward to monday mornings, your day easily gets absorbed in work, you are happy in your current job and you would not switch even if you get some more money, even without appreciation you get joy by just doing your work, you get to bed feeling fulfilled as you add value to the world doing your work. Then you are a person who is living your purpose.

Habit 6: A Purpose

Tip: Spend 15 minutes everyday doing what you love the most.See if that brings you joy and a purpose to wake up every morning.

Habit 7: Surrender To The Higher Power
When you accept things as they are or see God's hand in life situations miracles happen.

Always think positive even when life does not go the way we expected.

We might have done good things, put in all the hard work and spent all our money but when we don't get results we blame god, why bad things happen to good people.Take all the stress and have a victim mentality which inturn affects our health by stress.

Instead, we believe that God has a larger plan for us then we're unaffected by stress. Hence we achieve greater mental peace leading to ultimate health.

Surrender to the higher power" is a concept that appears in various spiritual and philosophical traditions, emphasizing the act of relinquishing control, trusting in a higher force or divine power, and aligning oneself with a greater purpose. Here are some key aspects and interpretations of surrender to a higher power:

Relinquishing Control:

- Surrender involves letting go of the need to control every aspect of life. It acknowledges the limitations of human understanding and control, recognizing that there are forces beyond our comprehension.

Trust and Faith:

- Surrendering to a higher power requires trust and faith in that power. It is a belief that there is a guiding force, whether it be a deity, the universe, or a cosmic energy, that is benevolent and has a greater plan.

Acceptance of What Is:

- Surrender is not resignation but acceptance. It involves acknowledging and accepting the present moment, even if it doesn't align with one's desires or expectations. It is about finding peace in the midst of uncertainties.

Letting Go of Ego:

- Surrender often involves letting go of the ego's need for control and recognition. It's a recognition that there is something greater than the individual self and that personal desires may not always align with a higher purpose.

Aligning with Divine Will:

- In many spiritual traditions, surrender is seen as aligning one's will with the divine will. It is an acknowledgment that there is a cosmic order or plan that is beyond individual understanding, and by surrendering, one seeks to harmonize with this higher order.

Freedom from Attachment:

- Surrendering often involves freeing oneself from excessive attachment to outcomes, possessions, or personal desires. It is about finding contentment and joy in the journey rather than being solely focused on the destination.

Practicing Humility:

- Surrender is a humble acknowledgment that humans are not all-powerful. It fosters a sense of humility, recognizing that there is wisdom in acknowledging one's limitations and seeking guidance from a higher source.

Devotional Practices:

- Surrender is often expressed through devotional practices such as prayer, meditation or rituals. These practices are a way of connecting with the divine and expressing one's openness to guidance.

Inner Transformation:

· Surrender can lead to inner transformation and a shift in perspective. By surrendering, individuals may find inner peace, resilience, and a sense of purpose that goes beyond individual desires.

Service and Compassion:

· Surrender is not passive; it often involves active engagement in serving others and acting with compassion. Surrendering to a higher power can inspire a sense of responsibility to contribute positively to the world.

It's important to note that the concept of surrender to a higher power can vary across different belief systems, and individuals may interpret it in ways that align with their personal spiritual or philosophical views. Whether it's seen as surrender to God, the universe, or a transcendent force, the essence often lies in cultivating a humble and trusting relationship with something greater than oneself.

Habit 7: Surrender To The Higher Power

Tip: Think Positive always. Remember that this too shall pass soon.Life is never a straight line, it's a roller coaster ride of ups and downs.There is a higher power and he has better plans for us.

4

Chapter 3

Importance Of Mindfulness

What is Mindfulness ?
Mindfulness is the natural ability to observe and dissolve
thoughts, emotions and behavior that arise in the present
moment without offering judgment and resistance.

We can observe that this is a natural ability for children. They are always in the present moment and they do not judge anyone which gives them the ability to learn and observe from the present moment and they are always in joy.

Judgment is something when we label something or someone good or bad or right or wrong.

Resistance is something which we say i don't want to; always and push away something. But the universe works this way.
What We Resist Persists

Always remember this life formula: **Judgment + Resistance = Suffering (Pain)**

So how do we not fall in the trap of pain? We simply practice being in the present moment by seeing and feeling things as it is without judgment.

Awareness is nothing but –

Mind: Identity,thoughts,perception,belief system
   Emotions: Feelings
   Body: Physical body
   Behavior: The way we react
   Experiences: Things that we are going through

Let's do some exercise of being in the present moment:

Sit in a place you feel comfortable and observe the things around you without any judgment for example I can see

1. Book shelf
2. Fan
3. My daughter's kitchen set etc.

Simply observe it as it is and now close your eyes.

-   Observe what you can hear. Simply be aware of the sounds around you
-   Next, observe how you feel on your body from head to toe.
-   Observe how you feel in your body if there is any heaviness just relax and say it's okay.

- Next go to your kitchen and eat something you like ,simply taste the food.
- Next observe the smell either from food or from your candle.

So from now on we will be aware of all the senses in the present moment without any judgment or thoughts. This will give our brain to tune into the present moment and be in the state of mindfulness which in turn helps us to be more joyful and not worry about what is going to happen tomorrow.

Being in the present moment, or practicing mindfulness, offers a wide range of mental, emotional, and physical benefits. Here are some of the key advantages:

Reduced Stress:

- Mindfulness helps break the cycle of stress by bringing attention to the present moment and reducing preoccupation with past or future events. This can lead to a calmer and more balanced state of mind.

Improved Mental Health:

- Mindfulness has been associated with reduced symptoms of anxiety, depression, and other mental health conditions. It encourages a non-judgmental awareness of thoughts and emotions, fostering emotional regulation.

Enhanced Focus and Concentration:

- Practicing mindfulness improves attention and concentration by training the mind to stay focused on the current moment. This can lead to increased productivity and better task performance.

Increased Self-Awareness:

- Mindfulness cultivates self-awareness by encouraging individuals to observe their thoughts and feelings without immediate reaction. This self-awareness can lead to a better understanding of one's own motivations and behaviors.

Better Emotional Regulation:

- By being present with emotions as they arise, individuals can develop a more skillful response to challenging situations. Mindfulness promotes a healthier relationship with emotions and reduces impulsive reactions.

Improved Sleep Quality:

- Mindfulness can contribute to better sleep by calming the mind and reducing racing thoughts. Mindfulness-based interventions are often used to address insomnia and sleep-related issues.

Enhanced Relationships:

- Being fully present in interactions with others fosters better communication, active listening, and empathy. Mindfulness can improve the quality of relationships by promoting genuine connection.

Greater Resilience:

- Mindfulness encourages a non-judgmental acceptance of the present moment, even in the face of challenges. This can enhance resilience and the ability to cope with life's ups and downs.

Improved Physical Health:

- Mindfulness has been linked to various physical health benefits, including lower blood pressure, improved immune function, and better cardiovascular health. The mind-body connection plays a crucial role in overall well-being.

Enhanced Enjoyment of Life:

- By being present and fully engaged in the current moment, individuals can derive greater satisfaction from daily activities and experiences. Mindfulness encourages a deeper appreciation for life as it unfolds.

Release from Overthinking:

- Mindfulness helps break the cycle of overthinking and rumination by redirecting attention to the present. This can lead to a quieter mind and a reduction in unnecessary mental chatter.

Cultivation of Gratitude:

· Being present allows individuals to notice and appreciate the positive aspects of life, fostering a sense of gratitude. Mindfulness encourages a focus on what is happening now rather than dwelling on what might be lacking.

These benefits highlight the transformative impact that mindfulness can have on various aspects of well-being. Incorporating mindfulness practices into daily life, such as meditation or mindful breathing, can contribute to a more fulfilling and balanced existence.

Now if you ask me if we follow this mindful meditation that is observing what we see,hear,feel inside, feel outside the body, our taste and smell we can be in the present moment which has so many benefits as mentioned above. The answer is yes, but we also must understand that we sometimes lose our cool and often we feel bad for getting too rough on other people or ourselves. Or sometimes visualize the bad things that happened to us and feel choked which is unnecessary. Ever wondered why ???

We all have a Pain Body who sometimes possesses us whenever we try to be mindful and be at the present moment and happy suddenly this pain body attacks us. Pain body loves pain.

So what to do when this happens is to simply identify when these negative past emotions flow,it is not me it is the pain body but I am stronger than the pain body. I cannot be easily possessed.

Here are few things that we could do to control the pain body:

1. Affirmations saying this is not me, it is the pain body

2. Cry it out and remember we cannot change the past.The power is in the NOW
3. Write how you feel and take a deep breath
4. Punch Pillows and let go
5. Yelling into a closed room

This way you can deal with the negative emotions and let go easily. Over time you will master to not be affected even when someone literally shouts at you, you will not lose your cool and you will know that it is his/her pain body.Without your entire day getting affected by this one incident.

To Identify The Pain Body

Pain Body=Anything and everything that does not feel blissful

Pain Body are of two types:

1. Passive Pain Body: Negative Thoughts
2. Active Pain Body: Attacks others and oneself, verbal abuse and negative self talk.

How To Release Pain Body ?

1. Take a deep breath
2. Ask yourself where you can feel the pain body
3. Locate the place and understand that it is not you, but the pain body
4. Take a deep breath and release the pain in your body.If it

doesn't go away, be strong and challenge it more.

5. The more aware that it is not you, but the pain body it weakens and finally dissolves.

This way you can deal with the negative emotions and let go easily.

7 things to ask when you have a negative emotion:
    A - Ask yourself is this problem really mine?
    B- Be responsible for your part
    C- Connect with your true source of inspiration
    D- Do not judge or resist
    E- Enjoy Life as it is
    F- Forgive to feel light and unload the bags that you have been carrying so far
    G- Get to the point where you realize that you are not these thoughts but you are just the awareness/witness.

When we die we do not carry anything with us except for the awareness/witness. Let go of Ego and you can easily become a mindful expert. Universe will unlock many doors and one such door is the pathway to wellness.

Ho'oponopono Prayer Miracle Story

Ho'oponopono is a traditional Hawaiian practice of reconciliation and forgiveness. The word "Ho'oponopono" can be translated as "to make right" or "to rectify an error." It is both a spiritual and therapeutic process that aims to restore harmony within oneself and in relationships with others.

The modern version of Ho'oponopono, often referred to as the "Ho'oponopono prayer," gained popularity through the work of Dr. Ihaleakalá Hew Len, a Hawaiian psychologist. He integrated the traditional Hawaiian practice into a simple and powerful mantra-like prayer.

The Ho'oponopono prayer is:
"I'm sorry.
Please forgive me.
Thank you.
I love you."

The story associated with Dr. Hew Len and Ho'oponopono involves his work at the Hawaii State Hospital in the 1980s. Dr. Hew Len was hired to work with mentally ill patients, many of whom were considered dangerous and were kept in a high-security ward. Instead of directly working with the patients, Dr. Hew Len practiced Ho'oponopono as a form of self-healing.

The essence of his approach was to take responsibility for everything in his experience, whether it was directly related to him or not. He believed that by healing himself, he could indirectly contribute to the healing of others and the environment.

The idea is rooted in the concept that our perceptions of the world are projections of our own thoughts and beliefs. By taking responsibility for those perceptions and working on inner healing, individuals can transform their experiences and contribute to positive change in their surroundings.

The story goes that, over time, the patients at the hospital experienced significant improvements. Violent incidents decreased, and some patients were eventually released. Dr. Hew Len's approach with Ho'oponopono was not based on traditional psychotherapy or counseling; rather, it focused on cleansing oneself of negative thoughts and emotions to promote healing and reconciliation.

While the story of Dr. Hew Len's work is compelling, it's essential to approach it with an open mind and understand that the effectiveness of Ho'oponopono can vary from person to person. The prayer itself serves as a tool for personal responsibility, forgiveness, and love, promoting the idea that healing starts from within.

5

Chapter 4

Powerful Pranic Healing Meditations

Pranic Healing is an energy healing system that originated from ancient esoteric practices and was modernized and systematized by Grand Master Choa Kok Sui. It is based on the concept that the body has an energy field, often referred to as the "aura," and that imbalances or blockages in this energy field can lead to physical, emotional, or mental ailments. Pranic Healing aims to cleanse and energize the energy field to promote overall well-being.

Here are the key principles and types of Pranic Healing:

Basic Principles:

- *Law of Self-Recovery*: Pranic Healing operates on the understanding that the body has an inherent ability to heal itself.

The role of the healer is to accelerate this natural healing process.

- *Law of Life Energy*: Pranic Healing is based on the recognition of the existence of life energy, also known as "prana" or "chi." This vital energy is essential for the well-being of the body and its various functions.
- *Law of Cleansing*: Pranic Healing emphasizes the removal of diseased or congested energy from the energy field to promote healing.

Pranic Healing Techniques:

- *Scanning*: Practitioners use their hands to scan the energy field, detecting imbalances, blockages, or areas of congestion.
- *Cleansing*: The removal of diseased or congested energy from the energy field is done through sweeping or cleansing motions.
- *Energizing*: Once the energy field is cleansed, fresh and vitalizing prana is channeled to the affected areas to promote healing.
- *Stabilizing and Preventive Healing*: Techniques to stabilize and strengthen the energy field to prevent future imbalances.

Types of Pranic Healing:

- *Basic Pranic Healing*: Focuses on the fundamental techniques of scanning, cleansing, and energizing to address a wide range of physical and psychological conditions.
- *Advanced Pranic Healing*: Expands on the basic techniques,

introducing specialized protocols for more severe or chronic ailments.

- *Pranic Psychotherapy*: Targets emotional and psychological issues by working on the energy field related to the emotions and the mind.
- *Pranic Crystal Healing*: Involves the use of crystals to enhance and amplify the healing process.
- *Pranic Psychic Self-Defense*: Teaches techniques to protect oneself from negative energy and psychic attacks.

Pranic Healing is taught in structured courses, and practitioners progress through various levels of training. The emphasis is on practical application, and students learn specific protocols for addressing different health conditions. It's important to note that Pranic Healing is not a replacement for conventional medical treatment but is often used as a complementary approach to support overall well-being. As with any alternative healing modality, individuals interested in Pranic Healing should seek guidance from certified practitioners or instructors.

Pranic Healing and Twin Heart Meditation should not be performed by people who are:

1. Heavy smokers
2. Alcoholics
3. Drug Addicts
4. People who are under stress
5. People experiencing anger or irritation at the moment when healing is required.

The patient may get worse after being healed since the energy bodies of these people are very dirty and may contaminate the patient.

If you want to become a good pranic healer, you can study the book, "The Ancient Science And Art Of Pranic Healing '' by Master Chao Kok Sui thoroughly and practice regularly. You will also have to eat only vegetarian food and completely avoid pork inorder to have a clean energy body.

The Twin Heart Meditation

The "Meditation on Twin Hearts" is a popular meditation technique developed by Grand Master Choa Kok Sui, the founder of Pranic Healing. This meditation is designed to promote physical and mental well-being, as well as to bring about inner peace and a sense of connection with universal energies. It typically involves blessing the Earth with loving-kindness and experiencing the energy of divine love.

Here's a simple narration for the Meditation on Twin Hearts:

Preparation:

- Find a quiet and comfortable place to sit with your back straight and your hands resting on your lap.
- Close your eyes and take a few deep breaths to relax your body and mind.

Invoke for Divine Blessings:

- Begin by invoking divine blessings. You can silently say, "I am that I am, I am not the body; I am not the emotions; I am not the thoughts. I am the soul."
- Visualize a brilliant light above your head, representing the divine energy or higher self.

Activate the Heart Center:

- Focus your attention on your heart center in the middle of your chest.
- Visualize your heart center expanding and glowing with a beautiful pink light, radiating love and compassion.

Blessing the Earth:

- Imagine the Earth in front of you, like a small ball.
- Send waves of loving-kindness to the Earth by visualizing a pink light radiating from your heart to envelop the entire planet.

Activate the Crown Center:

- Shift your attention to the crown of your head.
- Visualize a brilliant golden light above your head, representing divine energy pouring down into your body.

Downpour of Divine Energy:

- Allow the golden light to flow down through the crown center, filling your entire body with divine energy.
- Feel the divine energy cleansing your physical, emotional,

and mental aspects.

Experience Inner Stillness:

- Bask in the divine energy, experiencing inner stillness and peace.
- Be open to insights, guidance, or a deep sense of connection with the universal consciousness.

Closing:

- Gradually bring your awareness back to your physical body.
- Express gratitude for the divine blessings and the opportunity to bless the Earth.

Remember to practice this meditation regularly to experience its full benefits. The Meditation on Twin Hearts is known for promoting inner peace, reducing stress, and fostering a sense of interconnectedness with all beings. As with any meditation practice, it's essential to approach it with an open heart and mind.

There is a Youtube link in the reference below for Twin Heart Guided meditation you can also follow that.

6

Chapter 5

Getting Your Home Ready For Daily Satvic Lifestyle Tasks

It's important that our environment supports us in leading a satvic lifestyle to improve our wellness. There will be a lot of challenges that we will face while doing this and the only key is to be consistent and take it easy, don't do anything that you do not enjoy doing.

You can maybe do this during your off days. Once you set up your home it's very difficult to deviate.

Steps To Be Taken For Setting Your Home:

1. Write a sticky note saying why you want to follow a satvic lifestyle. It can be stuck where you often sit or see. The message can be,"Reversing Diabetes","Reversing Thy-

roid","Mental Peace" etc

2. A clock for setting up an alarm every morning at 5AM. Remember if we keep our alarm on the phone, probably we would start scrolling social media and that's the worst thing that we can do at the start of our day.

3. Having a healthy juice or having 2 big glasses of water. This way we are helping our prana shakti in cleansing.

4. Choose a place at home where you will be least distracted and buy a meditation mat or use your yoga mat if you already have.Do Twin heart meditation everyday or if you currently drink and smoke then do Light Meditation and avoid Twin heart meditation.

5. Check your fridge: Remove all the items which are bottled,tinned and canned. Check the ingredients behind if it is Red Label as we know it is harmful so we store it separately out of reach.

6. Avoid milk products like milk,paneer,butter and cheese.If you think this one is impossible then at least reduce the usage of these items. Try to replace cow milk by using Almond or coconut milk at home.

7. Buy Fresh vegetables and fruits and store them in your fridge. Arrange fruits in the dining table or living area where you often visit.

8. Buy Nuts and Seeds or you can buy mixed nuts and keep it in a transparent jar near the dining table or living area.

9. You can replace sugar with jaggery powder, dates and honey for sweetness.

10. Do not use Maida or maida products since it sticks in your intestine and it's not good for your Gut health.Replace maida biscuits/cookies by having fresh coconut slices or homemade cookies.

11. Replace chips packet with makhana it is a healthy replace-ment
12. Use coconut oil or olive oil for cooking your daily dishes if you are too addicted to refined oil taste than replace that with ground nut oil.
13. Avoid Tea and coffee. If it's too difficult to avoid this, switch to Herbal Tea and coffee made with hot water instead of milk or use almond or coconut milk.
14. Replace white rice with brown rice.
15. A prayer note to read every night before going to bed.

Once you have set up your home this way for your 21 days task in leading a satvic lifestyle to achieve wellness in life. Talk to your family or friends who live with you.They might have not been onboarded for this kind of lifestyle and they would think it is crazy to do such drastic changes. I too faced the same situation at my place.

But make them understand why you wanted to try this or make them read this book. But don't get demotivated or disappointed if you do not get a positive response, do not judge them saying that they need to have makhana instead of having masala chips. Instead you let them be how they wanted to be without judging or making them understand what is the right thing to do.You definitely follow this for 21 days to see if you could see any positive changes in your life.If yes, follow it for 3 more months and you will see miracles happening.

Once you have done these changes or most of the changes you are now fully ready to take up the daily 21 days task to improve your wellness in the path of satvic lifestyle.

7

Chapter 6

Your Daily Tasks for the Satvic Path To Wellness

Day 1: Sleep Early. Go to bed around 9:30 pm
   YouTube. Why 10pm Is The Best Time To Go To Bed

Day 2: Start Your day with Juicing and a powerful pranic healing twin heart meditation
   3 Healthy Morning Juice Recipes (Beginner Friendly)
   Master Co. (2017, May 26). *Abridged meditation on twin hearts* [Video]. YouTube. https://www.youtube.com/watch?v=N884j NJJpGc

Day 3: Make a satvic meal plan. I will give a sample meal plan so you can do what suits you the best.

Meal Plan

Morning:

- Juicing: ABC Juice for weight gain, white pumpkin juice for weight loss.

Breakfast:

- Fresh fruit salad with a variety of seasonal fruits (such as bananas, apples, berries, or melons).
- Whole grain cereal or oats with almond milk.
- A handful of soaked almonds or walnuts.

Mid-Morning Snack:

- Fresh coconut water or herbal tea (such as chamomile or mint).
- A small serving of dried fruits like dates or figs.

Lunch:

- Brown rice.
- Mung bean dal (lentils) or kitchari (a one-pot dish with rice and lentils).
- Mixed vegetable curry with seasonal vegetables.
- Lots of greens like spinach or kale.
- Fresh cucumber or tomato salad with a sprinkle of cumin and coriander.
- Yogurt (preferably plant-based) with a pinch of rock salt.
- Fresh fruit like papaya or pineapple.

Afternoon Snack:

- Herbal tea or fresh fruit juice.

- A handful of sunflower seeds or pumpkin seeds.

Dinner:

- Main Course:
- whole wheat chapati (Indian bread).
- Lightly spiced dhal or lentil soup.
- Steamed or sautéed seasonal vegetables.
- Side Dish:
- Raita (yogurt with grated cucumber and mint).
- Steamed broccoli or cauliflower with a drizzle of ghee.
- Dessert (optional):
- A small serving of sweet fruits like grapes or pears.

Evening Snack (optional):

- Fresh fruit or a small handful of nuts.

Before Bed:

- A cup of warm herbal tea, such as chamomile or lavender.

Notes:

- Emphasize fresh, seasonal, and organic produce.
- Avoid processed and overly spicy foods.
- Choose whole grains and avoid refined flours and sugars.
- Stay hydrated with water, herbal teas, and fresh fruit juices.

Remember that a Satvic lifestyle extends beyond just diet and includes other aspects such as thoughts, actions, and environment. It's always advisable to tailor any diet plan to your individual health needs and consult with a healthcare professional or nutritionist if necessary.

Satvic Movement. (2018, December 6). *This one diet can cure every disease | Subah Saraf | Satvic Movement* [Video]. YouTube. https://www.youtube.com/watch?v=xO5FBjz474g

Day 4: Have dinner by 7pm.

Day 5: Throw away all the packaged food in a box. If your family would not allow you to do this, ask them if you could shift this in a corner shelf out of sight so that you would not be tempted to have it.

Day 6: Join an exercise you love doing.

Take out 1 hour during your day for some physical movement and make it a habit by doing habit stacking.

Habit stacking is the one that you do everyday so you add a new habit after your existing habit so this way it's easy to follow.

Day 7: Start **_Ho'oponopono prayer_** whenever you can.

I Love You, I am Sorry, Please Forgive Me, Thank You.

Day 8: Have Gratitude, mindfulness and BE CONSISTENT

Day 9: Note down in a book.

- Habits I can begin Immediately
- Habits I am not ready for yet

Summary of 7 Habits:
Habit 1: Have a Clean Body (Have your dinner by 7pm)
Habit 2: Eat plant based food
Habit 3: Sleep like a baby
Habit 4: Let's move our body
Habit 5: Enhancing relationships
Habit 6: A purpose
Habit 7: Surrender to the higher power

Day 10: Write down a schedule for a week and stick it in your fridge and follow it for the next 21 days.

8

Satvic Lifestyle Wellness Test

Congratulations on completing the 21 days' tasks. It's time for the wellness score now.

This test was designed by the Satvic Movement Team by Subah Sarah and Harshvardhan who are my mentors and also the founders of The Satvic Movement.

I would request you to take a pen and paper and attempt this test.

The Ultimate Health Scans our Body,Mind,Heart and Soul.

If your answer is anyone of the below then give a score in a scale of 0 to 4

Never = 0	Sometimes = 2	Always = 4

1. My bowels get cleared in the morning everyday (your number based on Never, sometimes or always) –
2. I am in my ideal BMI –
3. I have a clear skin –
4. I feel energetic throughout the day –
5. I feel a strong sense of hunger 1-2 times a day –
6. I hit the bed and sleep within 5 minutes –
7. I experience no pain in the body –
8. I feel a general sense of Joy and find myself smiling at many occasions during the day –
9. I wake up in the morning excited –
10. I am able to let go of the unpleasant things that happens to me –
11. My mind is stable it is not easy for someone to make me angry or annoyed –
12. I feel genuine love for my close family and friends –

Your Total Score (*Add all the numbers*) =

Result:

0-24 = Low Health
25-36=Average Health
37-44=Great Health
45-48=Ultimate Health

What is your score =

What will you gain with Ultimate Health ?

1. Clean Body
2. Ideal weight
3. Radiant Skin
4. Tons of Energy
5. Deep Sleep
6. Strong Hunger
7. No pain in the body
8. Joy and Laughter
9. Excitement Each Day
10. Ability to Let Go Easily
11. Calm Mind, Even in Chaos
12. Genuine Love In Relationships.

9

Gratitude to my Masters and my Family

I would like to thank my masters who gave me the knowledge and support.

My Masters

Mr.Vanshit Upadhyay - For teaching me the skills on how to be an author

Ms.Subha Sarah and Mr.Harshvardhan- For the amazing knowledge on satvic lifestyle and its benefits

Ms.Karthika Nair - Mindfulness and visualization techniques were taught and complete guidance and support was given whenever i needed.

To all the spiritual masters and my family who stood as a back bone for me.

Special Thanks to my babe and my darling Daughter

I am always thankful to my mother. She is my biggest support.My brother is my role model and I am lucky to have a wonderful sister in law. My all time favorite is my niece. I am thankful to my mother-in-law and father-in-law for having faith in me.

Thanks to everyone and my readers who came so far.

To the supreme God.Thank you for your divine blessings.
For guidance,help,protection and illumination

10

References and Links

1. Fit Tuber. (2021, March 26). *How to Wake up Early Morning Daily? (and Not be Miserable)* [Video]. YouTube. https://www.youtube.com/watch?v=nVqguQH45gw

2. Satvic Movement. (2018a, January 19). *How to make Satvic Sabzi | Subah Saraf | Satvic Movement* [Video]. YouTube. https://www.youtube.com/watch?v=8U241PUvYOA

3. Yoga with Naveen. (2020, January 30). *9 Ways to practice mindfulness in Everyday life | Kartika Nair* [Video]. YouTube. https://www.youtube.com/watch?v=ruUAuQ-fDQo

4. Revolution By Light. (2011, October 19). *Importance of meditation* [Video]. YouTube. https://www.youtube.com/watch?v=9smvdQNzNa4

5. Revolution By Light. (2021, August 21). *Guided light channelling for schools* [Video]. YouTube. https://www.youtube.com/watch?v=A2pFF5PNBqo

6. AStudentofLife. (2020, August 21). *twin hearts meditation Master Choa Kok Sui* [Video]. YouTube. https://www.youtube.com/watch?v=vfAO_Qmx050

7. Mind Body Soul. (2022, October 7). *Ho'oponopono Prayer | 108 repetitions for Deep Healing & Forgiveness | Powerful Mantra Meditation* [Video]. YouTube. https://www.youtube.com/watch?v=lNeiLi882MU

8. *Buy The Ancient Science and Art of Pranic Healing book online at low prices in India | The Ancient Science and Art of Pranic Healing Reviews & ratings - Amazon.in.* (n.d.). https://www.amazon.in/Ancient-Science-Art-Pranic-Healing/dp/8192407705

The Lord Buddha

"Let us inspect our thoughts that we do no unwholesome deeds; for as we sow, so shall we reap."

We come to the end of this book and beginning of your journey.

I wish each one of you to be fully recovered from whatever you are going through and always be blessed and have a happy healthy life.

Kindly provide your valuable feedback for me.

Lot's Of Gratitude!!

With Love,
Vidya Arvind